MEET THE DINOSAURS!: WHEN REPTILES RULED

MEET THE GIANT DINOSAURS

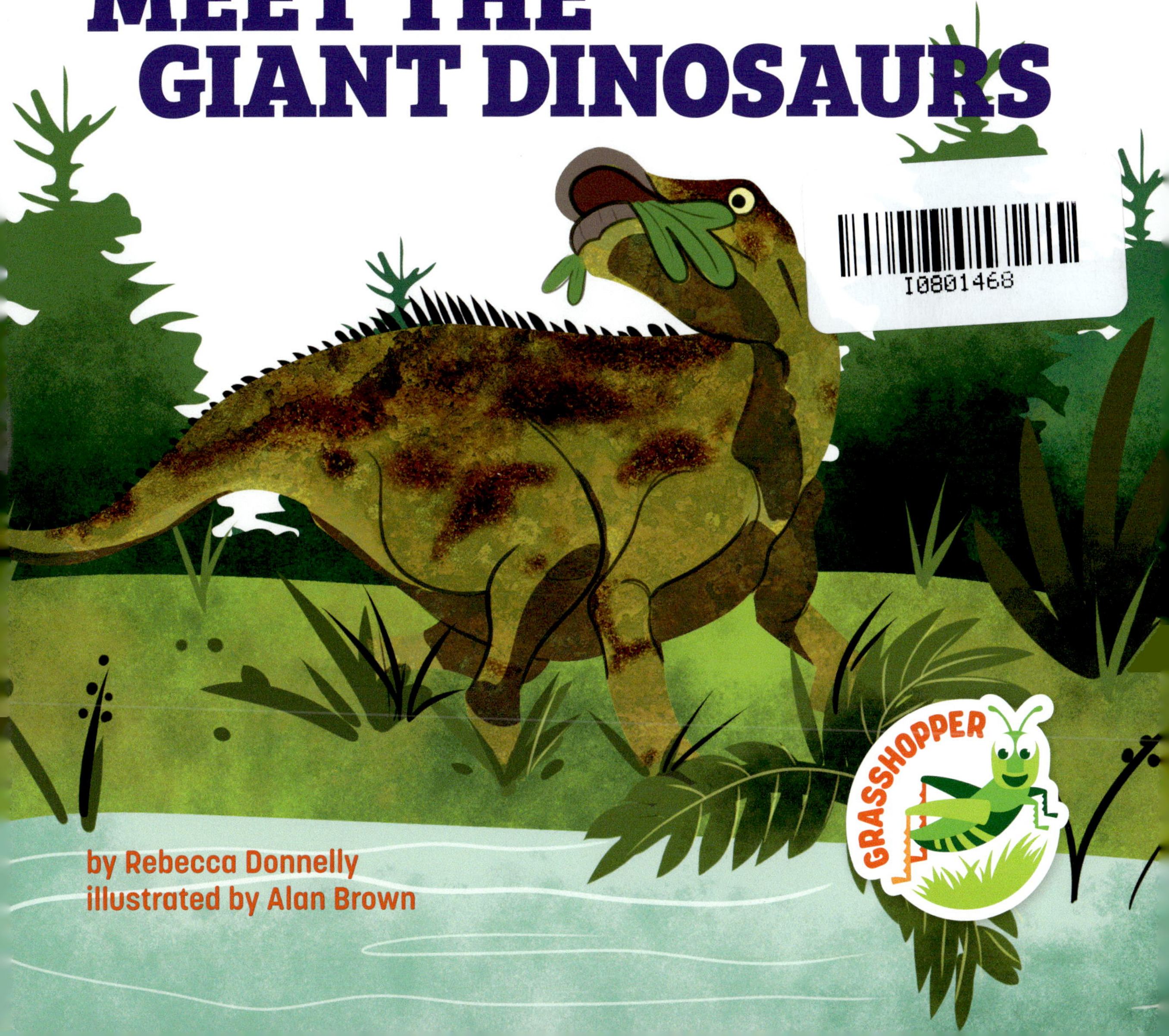

by Rebecca Donnelly
illustrated by Alan Brown

GRASSHOPPER

Tools for Parents & Teachers

Grasshopper Books enhance imagination and introduce the earliest readers to fiction with fun storylines and illustrations. The easy-to-read text supports early reading experiences with repetitive sentence patterns and sight words.

Before Reading

- Discuss the cover illustration. What do they see?
- Look at the glossary together. Discuss the words.

Read the Book

- Read the book to the child, or have him or her read independently.
- "Walk" through the book and look at the illustrations. What is happening in the story?

After Reading

- Prompt the child to think more. Ask: Some giant dinosaurs are carnivores. Some are herbivores. How do their sizes help them get food?

Grasshopper Books are published by Jump!
5357 Penn Avenue South
Minneapolis, MN 55419
www.jumplibrary.com

Library of Congress Cataloging-in-Publication Data

Names: Donnelly, Rebecca, author.
Brown, Alan, illustrator.
Title: Meet the giant dinosaurs / Rebecca Donnelly;
illustrated by Alan Brown.
Description: Minneapolis, MN: Jump!, Inc., [2022]
Series: Meet the dinosaurs!: when reptiles ruled
Includes index.
Audience: Ages 7-10
Identifiers: LCCN 2021037965 (print)
LCCN 2021037966 (ebook)
ISBN 9781636906089 (hardcover)
ISBN 9781636906096 (paperback)
ISBN 9781636906102 (ebook)
Subjects: LCSH: Dinosaurs–Size–Juvenile literature.
Classification: LCC QE861.5 .D6844 2022 (print)
LCC QE861.5 (ebook)
DDC 567.9–dc23
LC record available at https://lccn.loc.gov/2021037965
LC ebook record available at https://lccn.loc.gov/2021037966

Editor: Eliza Leahy
Direction and Layout: Anna Peterson
Illustrator: Alan Brown

Printed in the United States of America at
Corporate Graphics in North Mankato, Minnesota.

Table of Contents

Big Eaters 4
Timeline 22
Glossary 24
Index 24
To Learn More 24

Big Eaters

Hi! I'm Tracy the Tyrannosaurus rex. I'm one of the biggest dinosaurs of all time! Some of my cousins are bigger, but are they this scary?

I'm a carnivore.

Follow me while I hunt!

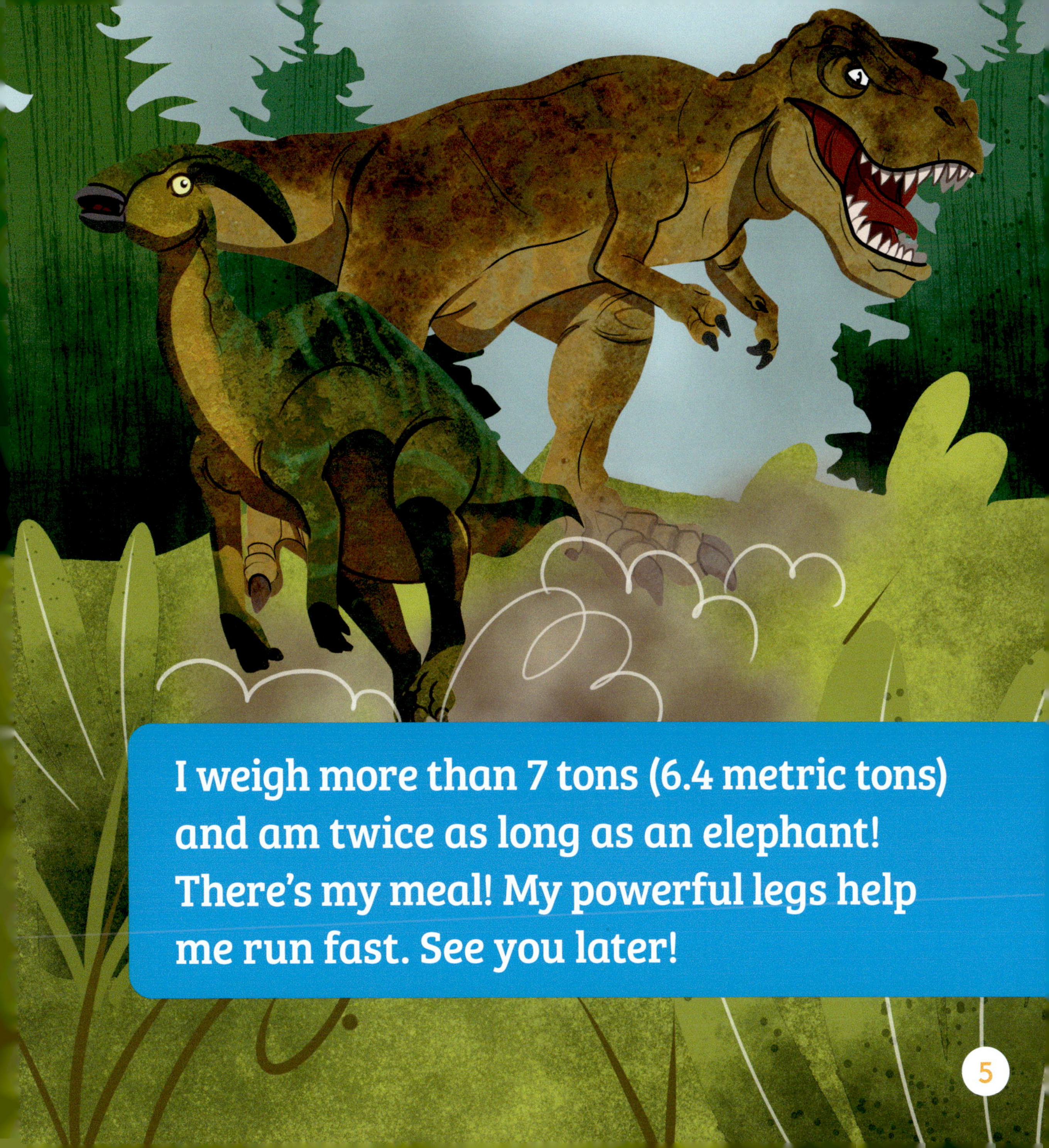

I weigh more than 7 tons (6.4 metric tons) and am twice as long as an elephant! There's my meal! My powerful legs help me run fast. See you later!

I'm Gina the Giganotosaurus. Tracy is my cousin, but I'm even bigger! I weigh more than 8 tons (7.3 t), and I'm 41 feet (13 m) long.

My long teeth are perfect for slicing into dinosaur flesh. Don't tell the other dinosaurs I'm on the hunt!

I'm Toby the Triceratops. "Tri" means three. I'm named for my three horns. I weigh just as much as Gina, and I'm almost as long. But does she have this cool bony frill or these horns? No way!

I have a sharp beak, too. I'm an herbivore.
I use my beak to cut plants to eat.

I'm Meg the Magnapaulia. I'm 49 feet (15 m) long.

I'm the biggest crested dinosaur. I make sounds that bounce around inside my crest. It acts like a megaphone so I can make really loud calls.

crest

I'm Shan the Shantungosaurus.
I'm the biggest hadrosaur.
Like all hadrosaurs, I have
a bill. My bill helps me
bite into tough plants.
Tiny teeth help me chew.

bill

I'm Sami the Spinosaurus. There are many kinds of marine reptiles, but I'm the only dinosaur that can swim. I have a snout like a crocodile's.

Gina and Tracy are big, but I'm the biggest carnivore ever. I love to catch fish!

You can call me Diego. I'm a Dreadnoughtus. I'm longer than any of these guys. I'm even longer than Tracy and Gina put together!

My neck is 37 feet (11 m) long. It lets me reach treetops to munch leaves. If a predator comes, I defend myself with my long tail.

I'm Brian the Brachiosaurus. I'm not quite as long as Diego, but I'm taller and heavier. I weigh as much as Sami and Diego put together! Diego has a longer neck, but I can reach even higher to find my dinner.

These other dinosaurs say they're big. But make way for me, Ana the Argentinosaurus. I'm 115 feet (35 m) long. I'm the largest land animal ever.

My giant friends and I are all extinct now. That's good news for you! One of my thighbones would be longer than you are tall!

Timeline

Dinosaurs lived millions of years ago. Take a look at when the dinosaurs in this book lived!

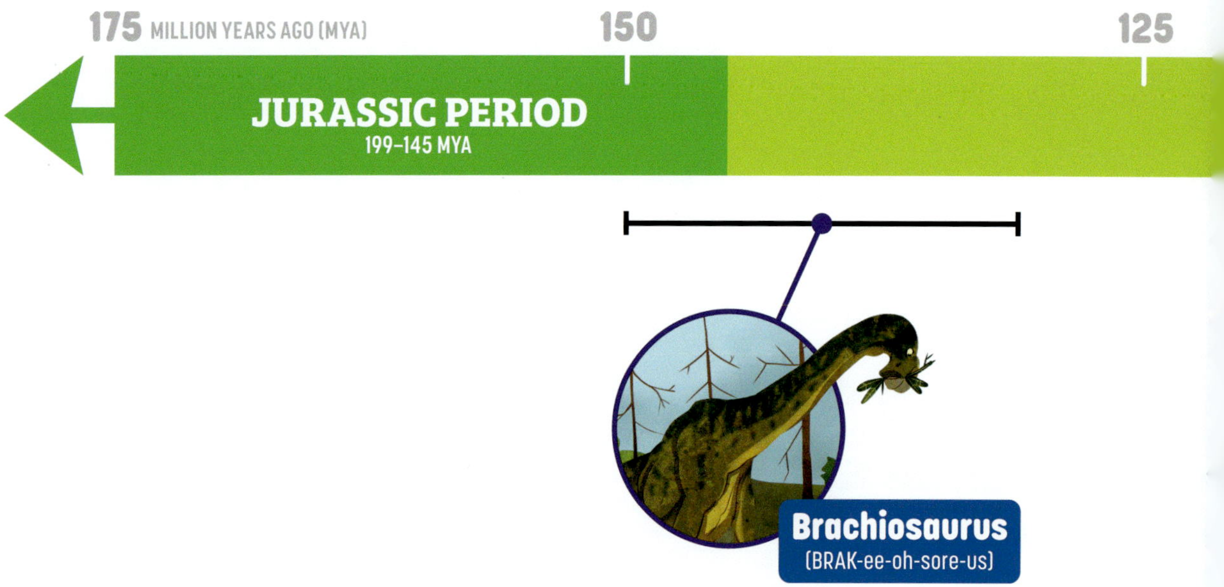

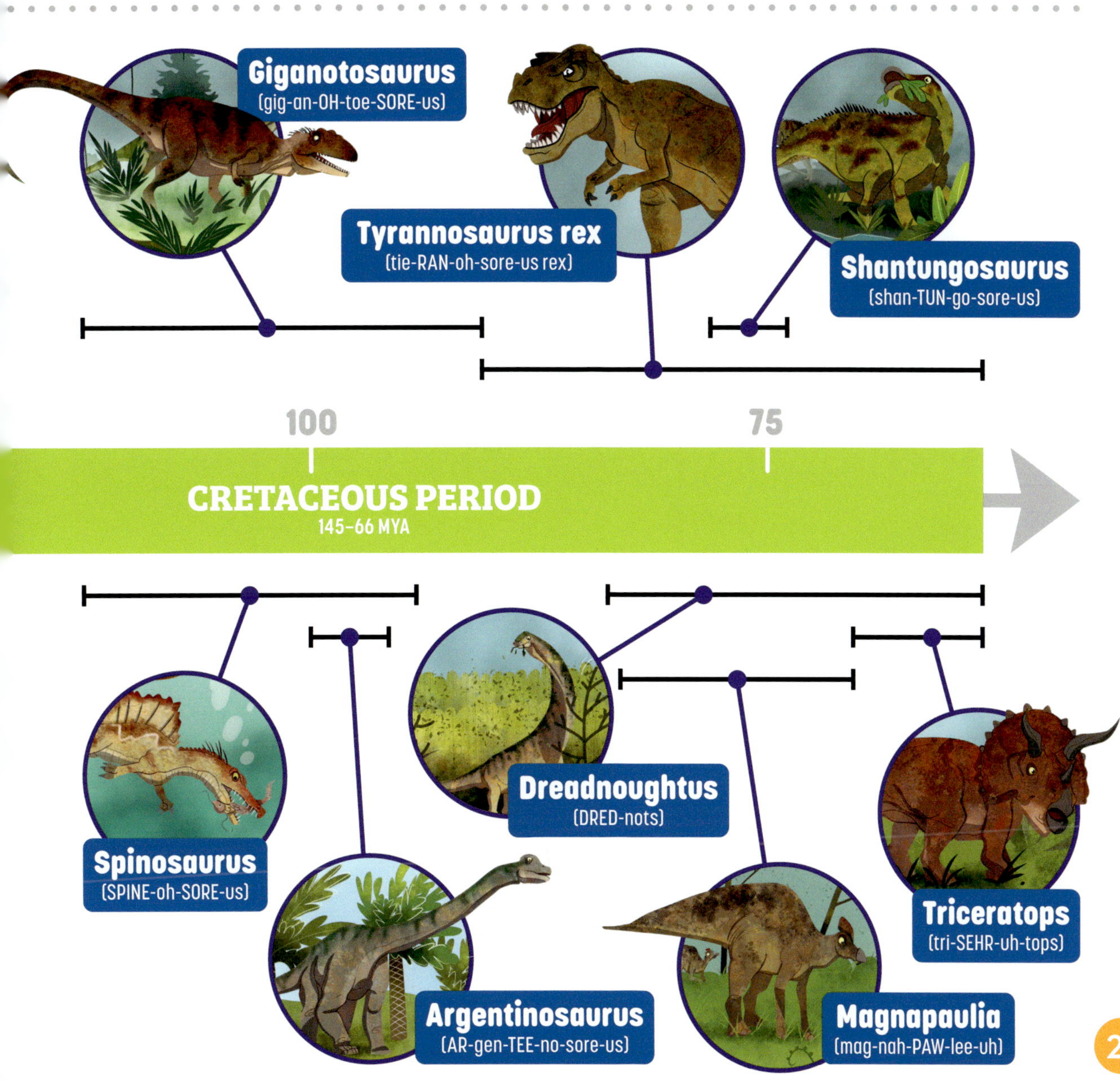
Giganotosaurus
(gig-an-OH-toe-SORE-us)
Tyrannosaurus rex
(tie-RAN-oh-sore-us rex)
Shantungosaurus
(shan-TUN-go-sore-us)
100
75
CRETACEOUS PERIOD
145–66 MYA
Spinosaurus
(SPINE-oh-SORE-us)
Argentinosaurus
(AR-gen-TEE-no-sore-us)
Dreadnoughtus
(DRED-nots)
Magnapaulia
(mag-nah-PAW-lee-uh)
Triceratops
(tri-SEHR-uh-tops)

Glossary

carnivore: An animal that eats meat.

crested: Having a narrow bony structure on the head.

defend: To protect from harm.

extinct: No longer found alive and known about only through fossils or history.

hadrosaur: A type of dinosaur with a long duck-like bill.

herbivore: An animal that eats plants.

marine reptiles: Animals that breathed air and lived in water but were not true dinosaurs.

megaphone: A device used to make the voice louder, sometimes shaped like a cone.

predator: An animal that hunts other animals for food.

Index

beak 9
bill 12
crest 10
frill 8
horns 8
hunt 4, 6
neck 16, 18
predator 16
snout 14
tail 16
teeth 6, 12
weigh 5, 6, 8, 18

To Learn More

Finding more information is as easy as 1, 2, 3.

1. Go to www.factsurfer.com
2. Enter "**meetthegiantdinosaurs**" into the search box.
3. Choose your book to see a list of websites.